Plant-Based Cookbook

New, Easy and Tasty Recipes for Vegan and Vegetarian Eating (For Beginners, On a Budget, Seasonal, For Two and More!)

By Jessica Weil

Table of Contents

Introduction

When you begin a plant-based vegan lifestyle you can be happy and satisfied in knowing that your choice will increase your health, decrease animal cruelty, improve the environment, and more. Many people find that this change helps them to lower their cholesterol, lose weight, improve their blood pressure, and even live longer healthier lives. Yet, sometimes it can be difficult to know what to eat when you see animal-based products and recipes all around you. Thankfully, there is no reason to worry! There are several healthy and delicious plant-based vegan recipes that you can enjoy. Whether you are interested in seasonal cooking, saving money on a budget, making meals for only two or beginner-friendly meals, you will be happy to find what you need within the pages of this cookbook.

It can be expensive to buy pre-made vegan options, but you can make your own at home that is just as delicious at a fraction of the price! After all, you can get many vegetables, tofu, and other ingredients at rather inexpensive prices. These ingredients can easily be made whether you are a beginner or experienced pro in the kitchen. Enjoying these foods within the seasons that they are traditionally grown will maximize flavor, nutrients, and also help your budget.

You don't have to allow a new lifestyle to stress you out or confuse you. If you are prepared with the knowledge and recipes found within the pages of this book, you will find that you can master the plant-based vegan lifestyle with ease. You will love the tasty meals, as will your family and friends.

Chapter 1: Breakfast

While the recipes within this chapter are perfect for breakfast, you can enjoy the day or night! These recipes are wonderful for either breakfast or "breakfast for dinner." Whether you are in the mood for muffins, carrot bacon slices, or protein-filled vegan quiches, you will love the recipes within this chapter.

Spring

This spring season is a bountiful time of year, full of carrots, asparagus, strawberries, artichokes, pineapple, radishes, mushrooms, rhubarb, and much more.

Carrot Bacon Slices

One of the great vegetables of the spring season is carrots. These are full of nutrients, flavor, and are incredibly versatile. In this recipe, you can even use carrots to make faux-bacon, perfect for all the health-conscious vegans who struggle to give up some of their favorite foods. While you can't expect this to be completely identical to "real" bacon, you will be surprised how it captures a similar flavor.

The Details:

- The Number of Servings: 2
- The Time Needed to Prepare: 10 minutes
- The Time Required to Cook: 15 minutes
- The Total Preparation/Cook Time: 25 minutes
- Number of Calories in Individual Servings: 151

- Protein Grams: 2
- Fat Grams: 11
- Total Carbohydrates Grams: 12
- Net Carbohydrates Grams: 11

The Ingredients:

- Carrot, large – 1
- Maple syrup – 1 tablespoon
- Tahini paste – 1 tablespoon
- Black pepper, ground - .25 teaspoon
- Liquid smoke – 1 teaspoon
- Light olive oil – 1 tablespoon
- Tamari sauce – 1.5 teaspoons
- Sea salt - .5 teaspoon

The Instructions:

- Peel the carrots and then slice them length-wise as thin as possible to make long strips.

- Add the maple syrup, tahini paste, black ground pepper, liquid smoke, light olive oil, tamari sauce, and sea salt in a small bowl and whisk them together until they form a thick marinade.
- Place the carrots and marinade together in a glass dish, tossing the carrots into the marinade so that they are fully coated. Once well-combined, allow the carrots to marinate on the counter for thirty minutes.
- While your carrots marinade allows your oven to preheat to a temperature of Fahrenheit four-hundred degrees.
- Line a cooking sheet with kitchen parchment or a sheet of silicone. Layout the marinated carrot strips on the prepared cooking sheet side-by-side, but not overlapping. Use a spoon to spread a

little extra marinade over the top of the carrot slices.

- Bake the carrot slices in the oven until they become crispy and bacon-like. This usually takes fifteen to twenty minutes, but it will vary slightly depending upon the thickness of the carrots and your oven. Remove the carrots from the oven and enjoy them alongside any of your favorite breakfast meals.

Strawberry Oat Bars

These oat bars are incredibly quick and easy to make, perfect for a special morning breakfast. You can enjoy these fresh out of the oven, or make them the night before if you want a grab-and-go meal in the morning. You won't believe how amazing these are with fresh in-season strawberries!

The Details:

- The Number of Servings: 3
- The Time Needed to Prepare: 10 minutes
- The Time Required to Cook: 15 minutes
- The Total Preparation/Cook Time: 25 minutes
- Number of Calories in Individual Servings: 367
- Protein Grams: 6

- Fat Grams: 15
- Total Carbohydrates Grams: 52
- Net Carbohydrates Grams: 48

The Ingredients:

- Rolled oats – .5 cup
- Strawberries, finely diced – 1 cup
- Corn starch – .5 teaspoon
- Light brown sugar - .25 cup
- All-purpose flour - .33 cup
- Lemon juice – 1 tablespoon
- Coconut oil, melted – 3 tablespoons
- Sea salt - .25 teaspoon
- Ginger, ground - .25 teaspoon
- Sugar – .5 tablespoon

The Instructions:

- Preheat your oven to a temperature of Fahrenheit three-hundred and seventy-five degrees before lining a regular loaf pan with kitchen parchment.

- In a small bowl for the purpose of mixing combine the light brown sugar, rolled oats, all-purpose flour, sea salt, and ground ginger. Once all of the ingredients are well-combined stir in the melted coconut oil, stirring again until all of the ingredients are well-integrated.

- Remove half a cup of the oat mixture and set it aside for later, pouring the remaining mixture into the bottom of your prepared loaf pan. Press the mixture into the bottom, until it is pressed in firmly.

- Sprinkle the finely diced strawberries over the oat mixture in the loaf pan, topping them off with a sprinkle of the cornstarch, sugar, and lemon juice. Once you finish adding these ingredients to the top of the strawberries, crumble the reserved oat mixture over the top.

- Place the loaf pan in the center of the oven and allow the strawberry oat bars to cook for twenty to twenty-five minutes until the crumble on top is golden in color.

- Remove the pan from the oven, allowing it to cool completely before cutting the contents into thirds.

Summer

The summer season is characteristic by fresh and vibrant flavors such as tomatoes, onions, corn, green beans, okra, figs, peppers, berries, melons, and more. These fresh flavors are wonderful when enjoyed in-season. This is best when grown at home or purchased at the local farmer's market, but you can also purchase these at your local supermarket.

Vidalia onion and Tomato Quiche

This vegan quiche is made with Vidalia onions and tomato for a sweet and acidic flavor that is unbeatable. You will find that the tofu filling gives it an abundance of protein and a wonderful creamy texture. The chickpea flour crust is gluten-free, nutrient-rich, and another protein-dense aspect you can enjoy about this dish.

The Details:

- The Number of Servings: 4
- The Time Needed to Prepare: 10 minutes
- The Time Required to Cook: 40 minutes
- The Total Preparation/Cook Time: 50 minutes
- Number of Calories in Individual Servings: 403
- Protein Grams: 29

- Fat Grams: 15
- Total Carbohydrates Grams: 40
- Net Carbohydrates Grams: 31

The Ingredients:

- Chickpea flour – 2 cups
- Olive oil – 1 tablespoon
- Sea salt - .25 teaspoon
- Ice water - .5 cup
- Firm tofu – 14 ounces
- White miso paste – 1 tablespoon
- Sea salt – 1 teaspoon
- Vidalia onion, thinly sliced – 1
- Tomatoes, large, thinly sliced – 2
- Nutritional yeast – 2 tablespoons
- Tamari sauce – 1 tablespoon
- Black pepper, ground - .25 teaspoon

The Instructions:

- Preheat your oven to a temperature of Fahrenheit three-hundred and fifty degrees. Then, in a bowl combine the chickpea flour, olive oil, .25 teaspoon of sea salt, and ice water together until it forms a dough. Press this dough into a pie plate so that it fully covers the bottom and sides in an even thickness.
- Place the prepared chickpea crust in the center of your preheated oven, allowing it to cook until the edges turn golden, about twenty minutes.
- Increase the heat of the oven to a temperature of Fahrenheit four-hundred degrees.
- Once the crust is done, the cooking, layer the thinly sliced tomatoes and onions into the bottom.

- In a blender or food processor pulse the remaining ingredients until completely smooth. Pour this mixture into the pre-baked chickpea crust and over the top of the onions and tomatoes.
- Place the quiche back in the oven, allowing it to cook until it becomes golden-browned over the top, about twenty to twenty-five minutes. Allow the quiche to cool for fifteen to twenty minutes before slicing and serving.

Autumn

Autumn is characterized by the warm flavors of squash, apples, pears, kale, beets, and mushrooms. These are not only full of flavor but also nutrition. You will love the ways in which these can be included in a variety of meals.

Spiced Pear Overnight Oats

These oats are delicious, perfect to make the night before you need them. However, you can also choose to make a large batch at the beginning of the week and enjoy a serving each day.

The Details:

- The Number of Servings: 2
- The Time Needed to Prepare: 10 minutes

- The Time Required to Cook: 15 minutes
- The Total Preparation/Cook Time: 25 minutes
- Number of Calories in Individual Servings: 342
- Protein Grams: 11
- Fat Grams: 9
- Total Carbohydrates Grams: 55
- Net Carbohydrates Grams: 46

The Ingredients:
- Chia seeds – 1 tablespoon
- Rolled oats - .5 cup
- Maple syrup – 2 tablespoons
- Soy milk, unsweetened – 1 cup
- Cinnamon – 1 teaspoon
- Pear, diced – 1
- Lemon juice - .5 teaspoon
- Maple syrup – 1 teaspoon

- Cinnamon - .5 teaspoon
- Pecans, chopped – 1 tablespoon

The Instructions:

- In a large glass jar combine the chia seeds, rolled oats, two tablespoons of maple syrup, soy milk, and one teaspoon of cinnamon. Seal the jar and allow it to chill overnight, or for a minimum of two hours.
- In a bowl toss together the remaining ingredients until the diced pair is well-coated. Immediately top it over the chilled and ready-to-eat overnight oats, or allow it to the first marinade for thirty minutes in the fridge.

Winter

Winter is a month for citrus, squash, Brussels sprouts, pomegranates, kale, parsnips, and persimmons. While it may not be as bountiful as other months, you can enjoy these ingredients while they are fresh, and you can enjoy preserved, canned, or frozen produce from the remainder of the year.

Roasted Persimmons Parfait

With this recipe, you can use whatever plain and unsweetened dairy-free yogurt you would like. There are many options, both store-bought and homemade. However, for this recipe, we like to use Plain Silk Almond Milk Yogurt.

The Details:

- The Number of Servings: 2
- The Time Needed to Prepare: 5 minutes
- The Time Required to Cook: 40 minutes
- The Total Preparation/Cook Time: 45 minutes
- Number of Calories in Individual Servings: 536
- Protein Grams: 8
- Fat Grams: 30
- Total Carbohydrates Grams: 63
- Net Carbohydrates Grams: 59

The Ingredients:
- Persimmons, ripe but firm – 3
- Honey, raw – 2 tablespoons
- Cardamom, ground - .25 teaspoon
- Water, hot – 1.5 tablespoons
- Sea salt - pinch
- Roasted walnut oil – 2 tablespoons

- Pistachios, roasted, chopped – 2 tablespoons
- Honey, raw – 1.5 tablespoons
- Vegan yogurt, unsweetened – 10 ounces

The Instructions:

- Begin by preheating your oven to a temperature of Fahrenheit three-hundred and seventy-five degrees. Then, place the hot water and two tablespoons of raw honey together in a small bowl, whisking them together until the honey is completely dissolved. Add in the roasted walnut oil and ground cardamom. Set the honey mixture aside.
- Peel the persimmons before cutting them into wedges, about one-inch in thickness. Toss these in the honey mixture and then place them on a baking sheet. Allow your

persimmons to roast in the oven for forty minutes until tender. Halfway through, flip the persimmon slices over, spooning the juice run-off back over the top of the fruit.

- Once the persimmons are done cooking combine together the vegan yogurt and 1.5 tablespoons of remaining honey. Divide the yogurt between two bowls; top them off with the persimmons and any remaining juice from the pan, and the roasted pistachios.

Chapter 2: Snacks

Snacks are an important aspect to plan into your diet. After all, if you do not have snacks planned, then you can resort to eating unhealthy options when you get hungry. Snacks can be simple foods such as fruits, nuts, and seeds. Yet, they can also be more complex for a real treat! But, even if a snack is more complex than grabbing a handful of nuts, it doesn't mean it has to take long to prepare or require too many ingredients.

Spring

Creamy Asparagus Tart

Believe it or not, but most puff pastry you buy at the supermarket is actually vegan! While homemade puff pastry usually makes use of butter, most mass-produced brands use oils. However, be sure to read the ingredient label before purchasing to ensure your chosen brand is one of the vegan options.

The Details:

- The Number of Servings: 4
- The Time Needed to Prepare: 10 minutes
- The Time Required to Cook: 15 minutes
- The Total Preparation/Cook Time: 25 minutes
- Number of Calories in Individual Servings: 193
- Protein Grams: 5
- Fat Grams: 13

- Total Carbohydrates Grams: 15
- Net Carbohydrates Grams: 12

The Ingredients:

- Puff pastry, vegan – 1 sheet
- Sea salt – .5 teaspoon
- Asparagus – 30 stalks
- Garlic, minced – 5 cloves
- Olive oil – 1 tablespoon
- Black pepper, ground - .25 teaspoon
- Cashews, raw - .33 cup
- Water – 3 tablespoons
- Apple cider vinegar - .75 teaspoon
- Lemon juice – 1 tablespoon
- Agave syrup - .5 teaspoon
- Sea salt - .5 teaspoon

The Instructions:

- Preheat your oven to a temperature of Fahrenheit four-hundred degrees and allow your sheet of puff pastry to thaw at room temperature for thirty minutes. Once it is thawed outlay it out on a cooking sheet. Using a fork poke holes into the center of the puff pastry, but leave about an inch around the edge of the puff pastry without holes.
- While the puff pastry thaws prepare your asparagus by snapping off the tough bottoms of the stems, which is usually about one-inch in length. Then, boil the asparagus in a pot of water for seven minutes until it is slightly tender. Remove the asparagus and allow it to cool.
- On a blender on high speed mix together the raw cashews, water, apple cider vinegar, lemon juice, agave syrup, and .5

teaspoon of sea salt until it is creamy, smooth, and thick. Spread this cashew cream onto the puff pastry, avoiding the one-inch border.

- Over the top of the cashew cream lay the boiled asparagus before brushing it with the olive oil. Sprinkle the black ground pepper, minced garlic, and .5 teaspoon of sea salt over the top of the asparagus.

- Bake the asparagus tart in the oven until the edges are puffy and golden, about fifteen minutes. Remove it from the oven and allow it to cool for ten minutes before slicing and serving.

Summer

Oven-Roasted Okra

This roasted okra is full of flavor, easy to make, and nutritious. Enjoy it on its own, or dip it in your favorite sauces and dips.

The Details:

- The Number of Servings: 2
- The Time Needed to Prepare: 5 minutes
- The Time Required to Cook: 40 minutes
- The Total Preparation/Cook Time: 45 minutes
- Number of Calories in Individual Servings: 166
- Protein Grams: 4
- Fat Grams: 10
- Total Carbohydrates Grams: 18

- Net Carbohydrates Grams: 12

The Ingredients:
- Okra pods, fresh – 24
- Cornstarch – 2 teaspoons
- Sea salt – 1 teaspoon
- Olive oil – 4 teaspoons
- Garlic powder – 2 teaspoons
- Cumin, ground – 2 teaspoons
- Coriander seeds, ground – 2 teaspoons
- Turmeric, ground - 1 teaspoon
- Black pepper, ground - .25 teaspoon

The Instructions:
- Preheat your oven to a temperature of Fahrenheit four-hundred and twenty-five degrees. While it heats up, wash the okra and dry it completely, ensuring no water remains.

- Cut the ends off of the okra pods, slice them in half, and then toss them in the olive oil in a kitchen bowl. Add in the spices and cornstarch, tossing until the okra is completely coated.
- Place the coated okra on a cooking sheet, placing the sliced side facing upward. Bake the okra in the center of the preheated oven until softened and slightly crispy. It should be smooth without much if any sliminess. If your okra is overly tough it is because the pods are too mature, so use young okra pods, if possible.

Autumn

Squash Fries and Garlic Chipotle Sauce

These fries are incredibly easy to make but have a unique and fun flavor. You can make them as you plan to eat them, or you can prepare a large batch, bake it halfway, and then flash-freeze it. Once frozen, you can remove one or two servings and cook them the remaining half of the time and enjoy them with the dipping sauce.

The Details:

- The Number of Servings: 2
- The Time Needed to Prepare: 7 minutes
- The Time Required to Cook: 30 minutes
- The Total Preparation/Cook Time: 37 minutes

- Number of Calories in Individual Servings: 147
- Protein Grams: 3
- Fat Grams: 9
- Total Carbohydrates Grams: 13
- Net Carbohydrates Grams: 12

The Ingredients:

- Delicata squash – 1
- Sea salt – .5 teaspoon
- Olive oil – 2 teaspoons
- Black pepper, ground - .125 teaspoons
- Vegan sour cream - .25 cup
- Soy sauce – 1.5 teaspoons
- Garlic powder - .25 teaspoon
- Dill, fresh, chopped - .5 teaspoon
- Paprika – pinch
- Chipotle hot sauce – 1 tablespoon

The Instructions:

- Preheat your oven to a temperature of Fahrenheit four-hundred and fifty degrees and then line a cooking pan with kitchen parchment.

- Slice the delicata squash in half, use a spoon to scrape out the seeds, and then slice the squash into half-moons each one-quarter of an inch thick. Once sliced, toss the squash in the sea salt, olive oil, and black ground pepper.

- Spread the seasoned squash out onto the cooking pan and allow it to roast until tender and browned about thirty minutes.

- Meanwhile, assemble the dipping sauce by whisking together the remaining ingredients. Once the squash is done cooking enjoy it hot by dipping it in the sauce.

Winter

Roasted Dijon Maple Brussels sprouts

These Dijon and maple roasted Brussels sprouts are accented with a smokey accent that makes them taste grilled. Yet, they are easily cooked within the oven, no grill required! You don't even have to enjoy these with a dip, as they are coated in so many flavors that they are perfect on their own.

The Details:

- The Number of Servings: 2
- The Time Needed to Prepare: 5 minutes
- The Time Required to Cook: 30 minutes
- The Total Preparation/Cook Time: 35 minutes

- Number of Calories in Individual Servings: 160
- Protein Grams: 4
- Fat Grams: 7
- Total Carbohydrates Grams: 22
- Net Carbohydrates Grams: 18

The Ingredients:

- Brussels sprouts, trimmed and sliced in half – .5 pound
- Olive oil – 1 tablespoon
- Sea salt - .5 teaspoon
- Maple syrup – 1.5 tablespoons
- Dijon mustard – 1 tablespoon
- Liquid smoke - .5 teaspoon
- Garlic, minced – 3 cloves
- Black pepper, ground - .25 teaspoon

The Instructions:

- Begin by preheating your oven to a temperature of Fahrenheit four-hundred degrees and preparing a cooking sheet by lining it with kitchen parchment.
- Toss the Brussels sprouts in the remaining ingredients until they are fully coated and lay them out on the baking sheet. Cook the sprouts until tender about thirty minutes flipping them over halfway through the cooking time.
- Remove the sprouts from the oven and allow them to cool for five minutes before enjoying.

Chapter 3: Entrees

The main portion of your meals, entrees is an important part of your meal plan. You want the entree of your meals to be filling and delicious so that you can enjoy them either on their own or with a few choice side dishes. No matter the harvesting season, you will love the entrees provided within this chapter.

Spring

Mushroom Leek Potpie

This potpie is quick and easy to make with the help of vegan puff pastry, meaning you don't have to spend time making a pie crust from scratch. Not only is this an easy option, but it also gives the potpie an amazing flaky and buttery flavor. Anyone would swear that this potpie is from a five-star restaurant rather than homemade.

The Details:

- The Number of Servings: 2
- The Time Needed to Prepare: 5 minutes
- The Time Required to Cook: 40 minutes
- The Total Preparation/Cook Time: 45 minutes
- Number of Calories in Individual Servings: 448
- Protein Grams: 15

- Fat Grams: 25
- Total Carbohydrates Grams: 41
- Net Carbohydrates Grams: 36

The Ingredients:

- Button mushrooms quartered – 17 ounces
- Leeks, trimmed and sliced – 2
- Olive oil – 1 tablespoon
- Garlic, minced – 3 cloves
- Sea salt – 1 teaspoon
- Tarragon, dried - .25 teaspoon
- Sage, dried, ground - .25 teaspoon
- Rosemary, dried - .25 teaspoon
- Marjoram, dried - .25 teaspoon
- Black pepper, ground - .25 teaspoon
- Puff pastry, vegan – 1 sheet
- Soy milk, unsweetened – 1.33 cup, plus 2 tablespoons
- Olive oil – 1 tablespoon

- Sea salt - .5 teaspoon

- All-purpose flour – 2 tablespoon

- Nutmeg, ground - .125 teaspoon

- Black pepper, ground - .25 teaspoon

The Instructions:

- Pour one tablespoon of the olive oil into a large Dutch oven pot along with the leeks and garlic, allowing them to cook for two minutes.

- Add in the button mushrooms, one teaspoon of sea salt, tarragon, sage, rosemary, marjoram, and .25 teaspoon of black ground pepper. Stir the ingredients together, cover the pot with a lid, and allow the ingredients to cook for eight minutes.

- Preheat the oven to a temperature of Fahrenheit four-hundred degrees and allow the puff pastry to thaw at room temperature.

- Meanwhile, in a saucepan combine the remaining olive oil and all-purpose flour, whisking them together. Once combined, slowly whisk in the 1.33 cup soy milk until it is smooth and thick. Add in the remaining seasonings and spices, allowing the mixture to cook until it is thick and bubbly.

- Add the prepared sauce to the pot with the now cooked mushrooms and leeks, stirring them together completely and turning off the heat of the stove.

- Pour the sauce and vegetable mixture into a nine-by-nine inch baking pan and then top it off with the puff pastry. Trim off any excess puff pastry before glazing the top with the remaining 2 tablespoons of soy milk.

- Allow the potpie to cook in the oven until the puff pastry is golden and flaky, about twenty-five minutes. Serve and enjoy immediately upon removing from the oven.

"Smoked" Carrot Dogs

These carrot dogs contain a surprising amount of protein, with twelve grams per serving! You can enjoy these just as you would traditional hot dogs, with your favorite toppings. These do require time to marinate, but it is well worth it with the flavor it adds.

The Details:

- The Number of Servings: 2
- The Time Needed to Prepare: 5 minutes
- The Time Required to Cook: 30 minutes
- The Total Preparation/Cook Time: 35 minutes
- Number of Calories in Individual Servings: 359
- Protein Grams: 12
- Fat Grams: 3

- Total Carbohydrates Grams: 69
- Net Carbohydrates Grams: 63

The Ingredients:

- Carrots, large, peeled – 4
- Tamari sauce – 3 tablespoons
- Maple syrup – 1.5 tablespoons
- Apple cider vinegar – 3 tablespoons
- Liquid smoke – 2 teaspoons
- Onion powder - .25 teaspoons
- Garlic, minced – 2 cloves
- Sea salt - .5 teaspoon
- Yellow mustard - .75 teaspoon
- Hot dog buns – 4

The Instructions:

- Peel the carrots and trim them so that they fit well inside of a standard hot dog bun. Place these carrots into a pot of boiling water, allowing them to cook for ten to fifteen minutes until they are fork-tender.

- Drain the carrots and rinse the boiling water off of them. Place the carrots into a plastic bag or another container.

- In a small bowl whisk together the tamari sauce, maple, apple cider vinegar, liquid smoke, onion powder, minced garlic, sea salt, and yellow mustard. Pour this sauce mixture over the carrots, tossing them together until the carrots are well-coated.

- Allow the carrots to marinate in this mixture in the fridge for four to six hours.

- After the carrots have marinated allow them to roast in an oven set to Fahrenheit four-hundred and twenty-five degrees for ten to fifteen minutes (until tender and flavorful) or grill them outdoors for about five minutes, until there are grill marks on all sides of the carrots.

- Serve the carrots on the buns, adding any of your favorite toppings that you desire.

Summer

Fresh Corn Chowder

This fresh and crisp summer chowder is full of summer produce, such as corn, zucchini, bell peppers, and more. Not only does this give the chowder an irresistible depth of flavor, but it also gives you balanced and healthy nutrition. This chowder is perfect to enjoy immediately upon cooking, or you can store it in the fridge or freezer to enjoy later on.

The Details:

- The Number of Servings: 2
- The Time Needed to Prepare: 5 minutes
- The Time Required to Cook: 35 minutes
- The Total Preparation/Cook Time: 40 minutes

- Number of Calories in Individual Servings: 416
- Protein Grams: 13
- Fat Grams: 6
- Total Carbohydrates Grams: 83
- Net Carbohydrates Grams: 71

The Ingredients:

- Red bell pepper, finely diced – .5
- Carrot, finely chopped – 1
- Onion, small, finely diced – 1
- Celery, finely sliced – 1 rib
- Golden potatoes, small, diced – 2
- Zucchini, medium, diced – .5
- Corn kernels – 2.25 cups
- Sea salt – 1 teaspoon
- Olive oil – .5 tablespoon
- Vegetable broth – 2.5 cups
- Soy milk, unsweetened - .75 cup

- Thyme, fresh – 2 sprigs
- Black pepper, ground - .25 teaspoon

The Instructions:

- Add the olive oil into a large Dutch oven pot along with the red bell pepper, carrot, onion, and celery. Allow these vegetables to cook until the onion begins to turn transparent, about eight minutes.
- Into the Dutch oven add the potatoes, thyme, and vegetable broth. Allow the broth to reach a simmer while the pot is covered with a lid, and then let it continue to simmer until the potatoes begin to become tender, about fifteen minutes.
- Once the potatoes begin to turn tender add in the corn and zucchini, uncovering the Dutch oven and allowing the chowder

to simmer for an additional ten minutes before removing the thyme sprigs.

- Into the Dutch oven add the soy milk and remaining seasonings before serving.

Thai-Style Zucchini Noodles

These Thai style noodles are full of flavors such as tamari, hoisin, and sriracha sauce along with fresh and fragrant garlic and cilantro. You will find these noodles are the perfect meal for two, full of flavor and nutrients. You only have fifteen minutes to prepare a meal? No big deal, as these noodles are incredibly quick and easy to cook!

The Details:

- The Number of Servings: 2
- The Time Needed to Prepare: 7 minutes
- The Time Required to Cook: 8 minutes
- The Total Preparation/Cook Time: 15 minutes
- Number of Calories in Individual Servings: 472

- Protein Grams: 15
- Fat Grams: 32
- Total Carbohydrates Grams: 37
- Net Carbohydrates Grams: 31

The Ingredients:

- Zucchini, medium – 2
- Carrots, large – 2
- Cilantro, fresh, chopped – 1 tablespoon
- Cashews, raw - .75 cup
- Lime juice – 1 tablespoon
- Tamari sauce – 1 teaspoon
- Sriracha sauce – 2 teaspoons
- Hoisin sauce – 1.5 teaspoons
- Peanut butter – 2 tablespoons
- Garlic, minced – 3 cloves
- Sea salt - .5 teaspoon

The Instructions:

- Peel the zucchini and carrots, and then using a vegetable spiralizer make the veggies into noodles. You want to make the carrots the smallest noodle size possible, whereas the zucchinis should be a medium-sized noodle. If you don't have a vegetable spiralizer you can use a peeler to make the noodles, instead. Set the carrots and zucchini aside.
- Into a large skillet whisk together the tamari sauce, peanut butter, minced garlic, sriracha sauce, hoisin sauce, and lime juice. Allow the sauce to cook over medium heat for two minutes until the garlic is fragrant.
- Into the skillet add the vegetable "noodles" and raw cashews, tossing the ingredients together so that the vegetables are fully covered in the sauce.

Continue to toss and stir the ingredients while they cook and soften, requiring about five minutes.

- Once the noodles are al dente and tender to your preference toss in the cilantro and serve the noodles immediately.

Autumn

Quinoa and Kale Pilaf

Not only is this dish incredibly easy to cook, but it is also full of essential nutrients. You are able to attain a balance of healthy protein, fats, and carbohydrates, as well as vitamins and minerals. Whether you are enjoying this entree with a fancy dinner or for lunch at the office, you are sure to love the deep autumnal flavors.

The Details:
- The Number of Servings: 2
- The Time Needed to Prepare: 5 minutes
- The Time Required to Cook: 11 minutes
- The Total Preparation/Cook Time: 16 minutes

- Number of Calories in Individual Servings: 393
- Protein Grams: 10
- Fat Grams: 23
- Total Carbohydrates Grams: 38
- Net Carbohydrates Grams: 32

The Ingredients:
- Quinoa, cooked – 1.75 cups
- Olive oil – 1.5 tablespoons
- Mushrooms, sliced – 1 cup
- Kale, chopped – 1 cup
- Green onions, chopped – 2 tablespoons
- Walnuts, chopped - .25 cup
- Sea salt - .5 teaspoon

The Instructions:
- Cook the quinoa according to the directions on the package. Meanwhile,

place the olive oil and mushrooms in a medium-large skillet and allow them to sauté over medium heat for three minutes. Add in the kale, allowing the vegetables to cook for an additional three minutes.

- Once the quinoa is cooked, add it to the vegetable skillet along with the walnuts, green onions, and seasonings. Allow the pilaf to toast for an additional five minutes until the quinoa is a little crispy.

- Remove the skillet from the heat and serve on its own or with your favorite sides.

Creamy Sweet Potato Pasta Casserole

This pasta dish is the perfect creamy meal for a cold autumn night. You will love how smooth and creamy it is, all while being dairy-free. Enjoy this pasta alone, or serve it in smaller servings to enjoy it along with a side dish.

The Details:

- The Number of Servings: 4
- The Time Needed to Prepare: 10 minutes
- The Time Required to Cook: 25 minutes
- The Total Preparation/Cook Time: 35 minutes
- Number of Calories in Individual Servings: 559
- Protein Grams: 20
- Fat Grams: 11
- Total Carbohydrates Grams: 93

- Net Carbohydrates Grams: 87

The Ingredients:
- Penne pasta, dry – 3 cups
- Bread crumbs – 1 cup
- Mushrooms, button, diced – 3
- Green onions, diced – 2
- Red bell pepper, diced – 1
- Italian herb seasoning – 1 teaspoon
- Paprika, smoked – 1 teaspoon
- Sweet potato, large, diced – 1
- Tahini paste – 2 tablespoons
- Nutritional yeast – 2 tablespoons
- Garlic, minced – 3 cloves
- Olive oil – 2 teaspoons
- Lemon juice – 2 teaspoons
- Sea salt – teaspoon
- Soy milk – 1 cup

The Instructions:

- Prepare the pasta according to the directions on the package and then set it aside.

- Meanwhile, peel the sweet potato and boil it in water until it is fork-tender, about ten to fifteen minutes. Drain off the water, and rinse the potato under cold water.

- In a skillet, sauté the bell pepper, onion, green onion, and olive oil until the onion and pepper are tender, about five minutes.

- In a blender combine the sautéed vegetables, sweet potato, herb seasoning, paprika, tahini paste, nutritional yeast, garlic, sea salt, and soy milk. If the sauce is overly thick you can add a small amount of water. Blend the sauce until it is creamy and smooth.

- Place the cooked pasta and prepared sauce into a large nine-by-thirteen inch baking dish, stirring them until the pasta is fully coated in the sauce. Top it off with the bread crumbs and allow it to cook under the oven's broiler until golden, about two to three minutes.

Winter

Butternut and Arugula Pizza

This pizza is incredibly easy to make, as you can simply use a pre-made crust from the grocery store and vegan mozzarella-style shreds. For this recipe, we like to use Daiya dairy-free cheese. However, you can use whatever brand you prefer or homemade. Just keep in mind that changes in the brand will alter the nutritional information slightly.

The Details:

- The Number of Servings: 3
- The Time Needed to Prepare: 10 minutes
- The Time Required to Cook: 15 minutes
- The Total Preparation/Cook Time: 25 minutes

- Number of Calories in Individual Servings: 465
- Protein Grams: 9
- Fat Grams: 19
- Total Carbohydrates Grams: 64
- Net Carbohydrates Grams: 60

The Ingredients:

- Pizza crust, prepared, vegan – 1
- Butternut squash, pureed – 1 cup
- Black pepper, ground - .125 teaspoon
- Olive oil – 1 tablespoon
- Sea salt - .5 teaspoon
- Arugula – 1 cup
- Garlic, minced – 4 cloves
- Red onion, medium, thinly sliced – 1
- Olive oil – 1 tablespoon
- Walnuts, toasted, chopped – 2 tablespoons

- Balsamic reduction glaze – 2 tablespoons
- Vegan mozzarella shreds - .5 cup

The Instructions:

- Preheat your oven to a temperature of Fahrenheit four-hundred degrees and prepare a cooking sheet, preferably around one specifically for pizza.

- For the squash puree, you can use either fresh or cooked butternut squash or frozen options. Combine the puree with the black pepper, 1 tablespoon of olive oil, and sea salt before setting it aside.

- With the remaining 1 tablespoon of olive oil sauté the garlic and onion until slightly translucent and browned, about five to seven minutes over medium heat. Remove the skillet from the stove.

- Place the prepared pizza crust on the cooking sheet and then spread the pureed butternut sauce over the top. Add the garlic and onions and then sprinkle the dairy-free cheese over everything.
- Allow the pizza to bake in the preheated oven until the vegan cheese is melted, about ten minutes.
- Remove the butternut pizza from the oven and top it with the arugula, toasted walnuts, and balsamic reduction/glaze. Slice the pizza into six pieces and then serve.

Butternut Squash Risotto

This risotto is incredibly easy to cook; you won't believe that you can have risotto of this quality made within your own kitchen. The butternut squash is wonderfully accented by the nutmeg, white wine, and nutritional yeast. However, if you do not have the time to cook and puree a squash, you can instead choose to use canned pumpkin puree.

The Details:

- The Number of Servings: 2
- The Time Needed to Prepare: 4 minutes
- The Time Required to Cook: 36 minutes
- The Total Preparation/Cook Time: 40 minutes
- Number of Calories in Individual Servings: 412

- Protein Grams: 7
- Fat Grams: 10
- Total Carbohydrates Grams: 71
- Net Carbohydrates Grams: 68

The Ingredients:

- Butternut squash puree (or pumpkin puree) - .25 cup
- Vegetable broth – 2 to 3 cups
- White wine – 2 tablespoons
- Onion, finely diced – .5
- Olive oil – 1.5 tablespoons
- Arborio rice – .75 cup
- Black pepper, ground - .25 teaspoon
- Garlic, minced – 3 cloves
- Nutmeg - .125 teaspoon
- Nutritional yeast – 1 tablespoon
- Sea salt – .75 teaspoon

The Instructions:

- Add the olive oil to a large Dutch oven over medium-high heat and allow the onions to cook in the oil until they become transparent about four minutes. Add in the garlic and cook the mixture for an additional two minutes.

- Add the rice to the pot and toast it for a minute before adding in the wine. Allow the wine to evaporate before slowly adding in half a cup of the vegetable broth. Continue slowly adding the broth, only half a cup at a time, allowing it to absorb into the rice completely each time before you add in the next portion of broth.

- Allow the risotto to cook until the rice is al dente, about twenty to thirty minutes.

If needed, you can add more broth as it cooks.

- Once the risotto is almost done cooking stir in the butternut squash puree, seasonings, and nutritional yeast. Serve the risotto immediately.

Parsnip Pear Soup

This soup is easy to make, yet full of flavor! Parsnips really don't get enough love, but paired with fresh herbs and pears they make a wonderful soup.

The Details:

- The Number of Servings: 2
- The Time Needed to Prepare: 5 minutes
- The Time Required to Cook: 35 minutes
- The Total Preparation/Cook Time: 40 minutes
- Number of Calories in Individual Servings: 326
- Protein Grams: 4
- Fat Grams: 7
- Total Carbohydrates Grams: 63
- Net Carbohydrates Grams: 51

The Ingredients:

- Leek, sliced – 1
- Bartlett pears, sliced – 1
- Olive oil – 1 tablespoon
- Parsnips, sliced – 3
- Sea salt – 1 teaspoon
- Vegetable broth – 2 cups
- Thyme, fresh – 5 sprigs
- Bay leaf – 1
- Black pepper, ground - .125 teaspoon

The Instructions:

- Preheat your oven to a temperature of Fahrenheit four-hundred degrees and line a cooking sheet with kitchen parchment. On this pan add the sliced parsnips and pears. Toss these with half of the olive oil and bake until slightly tender and browned about fifteen to twenty minutes.

- With the remaining half of the olive oil sauté the leek on the stove for five minutes before adding in the oven-roasted parsnips and peas, bay leaf, thyme, and vegetable broth. Allow this mixture to reach a boil before reducing the heat and allowing it to simmer for twenty minutes.

- Remove the thyme and bay leaves from the soup and then blend it in a large blender or with a hand-held stick blender. Serve immediately alone or with freshly-made croutons.

Chapter 4: Sides

Side dishes help to make dinner more fun by giving you more options of what to enjoy. Not only that, but they can also help to balance out your meals, increasing your nutrition. Whether it is spring, summer, autumn, or winter you will find these side dishes to die for.

Spring

Creamy Avocado Potato Salad

This delicious and creamy potato salad is much healthier than your average varieties, as it uses the fat of the avocado rather than mayonnaise. These fats have been proven to have amazing health benefits, and when paired with the other vegetables and herbs you have a flavorful, delicious, and healthy side dish.

The Details:

- The Number of Servings: 2
- The Time Needed to Prepare: 5 minutes
- The Time Required to Cook: 10 minutes
- The Total Preparation/Cook Time: 15 minutes
- Number of Calories in Individual Servings: 238
- Protein Grams: 4
- Fat Grams: 14

- Total Carbohydrates Grams: 25
- Net Carbohydrates Grams: 16

The Ingredients:

- Avocados – 1
- Yukon Gold potatoes - .66 pound
- Dill, fresh, chopped – 1 tablespoon
- Scallion, chopped – 1
- Chives, fresh, chopped – 1 tablespoon
- Peas, frozen and thawed - .33 cup
- Sea salt - .25 teaspoon
- Lime juice – 2 teaspoons
- Red pepper flakes – .125 teaspoon

The Instructions:

- Wash the potatoes and slice those pieces about one-quarter of an inch thick each. Place these potatoes in a pot covering them with water and a generous amount of salt, and then allow the pot to come to a boil on the stove. Once boiling, allow the potatoes to cook until fork-tender, about ten minutes. Once done, drain off the water and allow the heat of the potatoes to let the excess liquid evaporate.

- Meanwhile, slice the avocado in half and remove the pit. Scoop out the flesh of the fruit and add it to a medium-sized kitchen bowl. Using a fork mash the avocado along with the lime juice. Stir in the scallions and seasonings.

- Into the bowl with the avocado mixture add the cooked potatoes and the green beans, using a spatula to gently toss the ingredients together without breaking the potatoes too much. Taste and adjust the seasonings to your preference and then serve.

Summer

Miso Glazed Eggplant

This eggplant is full of flavor and unique, as it has a delicious Japanese miso glaze with garlic, ginger, and sesame seeds. If you haven't enjoyed eggplant in the past, I highly recommend trying this recipe. Many people are unaware of how to prepare eggplant to remove its bitterness, but this recipe walks you through the process with ease.

The Details:

- The Number of Servings: 2
- The Time Needed to Prepare: 7 minutes
- The Time Required to Cook: 17 minutes
- The Total Preparation/Cook Time: 24 minutes

- Number of Calories in Individual Servings: 220
- Protein Grams: 5
- Fat Grams: 9
- Total Carbohydrates Grams: 31
- Net Carbohydrates Grams: 22

The Ingredients:

- Eggplant – 1
- Miso paste – 1.5 tablespoon
- Sugar – 1.5 tablespoons
- Rice vinegar – 1 tablespoon
- Tamari sauce – 2 teaspoons
- Olive oil – 1 tablespoon
- Garlic, minced – 2 cloves
- Sea salt - .5 teaspoon
- Ginger, fresh, grated – 1 tablespoon
- Sesame seeds – 2 teaspoons

The Instructions:

- Into a small saucepan add the miso, sugar, vinegar, garlic, ginger, tamari sauce, and sea salt. Allow this to cook over low heat for a couple of minutes, until it becomes shiny and the sugar is melted. Remove it from the heat and set it aside.

- Slice the eggplant in half lengthwise and then use the knife to score the flesh of the eggplant diagonally along with the fruit. The appearance should resemble grill marks. Soak this in a bowl of water for five minutes to remove the bitterness.

- After the eggplant has finished soaking remove it from the water and dry it off with a clean kitchen towel. Wrap the eggplant with plastic wrap and then microwave it for five minutes.

- Preheat the oven to a temperature of Fahrenheit four-hundred degrees. While it preheats add the oil to an oven-safe large skillet, placing the eggplant flesh-side down and allowing it to sear for about five minutes.
- Flip the eggplant over so that the flesh-side is facing upward and then glaze the vegetable with the prepared miso sauce. Place the skillet in the oven, allowing it to cook for an additional five minutes with the glaze.
- Remove the eggplant from the oven and top it off with the sesame seeds before serving.

Autumn

Maple Roasted Beets and Carrots

These sweet and savory roasted root vegetables
are the perfect accompaniment to any meal.
You will find that the maple is perfectly
accented by the nutty tahini paste, giving these
beets an unbeatable flavor.

The Details:
- The Number of Servings: 2
- The Time Needed to Prepare: 10 minutes
- The Time Required to Cook: 15 minutes
- The Total Preparation/Cook Time: 25
  minutes
- Number of Calories in Individual
  Servings: 223
- Protein Grams: 3

- Fat Grams: 11
- Total Carbohydrates Grams: 29
- Net Carbohydrates Grams: 23

The Ingredients:

- Beets, medium, peeled and diced – 2
- Carrots, large, peeled and sliced – 3
- Olive oil – 1 tablespoon
- Sea salt – .5 teaspoon
- Tahini paste – 1 tablespoon
- Maple syrup – 1.5 tablespoons
- Black pepper, ground - .125 teaspoon

The Instructions:

- Preheat your oven to a temperature of Fahrenheit four-hundred and twenty-five degrees and prepare a cooking sheet for the vegetables.

- After cutting the beets and carrots into slices approximately the same size places them on the prepared baking sheet. Over the top of the vegetables drizzle the olive oil, sea salt, and black pepper, tossing the ingredients so that they are fully coated.
- Spread the vegetables out into an even layer so that they cook evenly, and then roast them until they are beginning to turn tender, but are still kind of crispy about fifteen minutes.
- Remove the baking sheet from the oven and toss the vegetables in the maple syrup and tahini paste before returning it to the oven for five additional minutes. Remove once the maple is caramelized and the vegetables are tender, and then serve.

Winter

Brussels Sprout and Apple Salad

This salad is incredibly quick and easy to prepare, but it will wow a crowd into thinking that you have assembled something time-consuming. This is perfect for when you want to impress guests or simply are looking to enjoy a delicious side to your main meal.

The Details:

- The Number of Servings: 2
- The Time Needed to Prepare: 10 minutes
- The Time Required to Cook: 15 minutes
- The Total Preparation/Cook Time: 25 minutes
- Number of Calories in Individual Servings: 250

- Protein Grams: 9
- Fat Grams: 13
- Total Carbohydrates Grams: 28
- Net Carbohydrates Grams: 17

The Ingredients:

- Brussels sprouts stem removed - .5 pound
- Red apple, medium, diced – 1
- Almonds, chopped, toasted - .25 cup
- Sesame seeds, toasted – 2 tablespoons
- Balsamic vinegar – 2 teaspoons
- Lemon juice – 1 teaspoon
- Tahini paste – 2 teaspoons
- Ginger, ground - .25 teaspoon
- Cinnamon, ground - .25 teaspoon
- Sea salt - .5 teaspoon
- Red pepper flakes - .125 teaspoon
- Water – 1 tablespoon

The Instructions:

- In the medium-sized kitchen, bowl whisks together the vinegar, lemon juice, tahini, ginger, cinnamon, salt, red pepper flakes, and water until well-combined. Set the dressing aside.

- Using the shredding attachment on your food processor slice up the Brussels sprouts. Add them to the dressing bowl along with the sliced apples, almonds, and sesame seeds. Toss all of the ingredients together and then serve.

Chapter 5: Desserts

In this chapter, you will find desserts you can enjoy on the plant-based vegan diet. Just because you are avoiding dairy and eggs doesn't mean you can't enjoy some of your favorite treats! Rather than just making these desserts vegan, we are making them even better before by adding it tasty ingredients that perfectly accent each recipe.

Chocolate Chunk Tahini Cookies

These cookies are much better than your average chocolate chip cookies. Not only do these contain less sugar, but they also have tahini paste, which complements the chocolate with an irritable nutty flavor.

The Details:

- The Number of Servings: 12
- The Time Needed to Prepare: 5 minutes
- The Time Required to Cook: 12 minutes
- The Total Preparation/Cook Time: 17 minutes
- Number of Calories in Individual Servings: 236
- Protein Grams: 3
- Fat Grams: 15
- Total Carbohydrates Grams: 22
- Net Carbohydrates Grams: 20

The Ingredients:

- Tahini paste - .25 cup
- Soy milk – 2 tablespoons
- Brown sugar, packed – 3 tablespoons
- Sugar – 3 tablespoons
- Coconut oil - .25 cup

- Sea salt - .5 teaspoon
- Vanilla extract - .5 teaspoon
- Cornstarch – 1 tablespoon
- Baking soda - .25 teaspoon
- Baking powder - .25 teaspoon
- All-purpose flour - .66 cup
- Dark chocolate, 60-70%, chopped into chunks – 1.33 cup

The Instructions:

- Using a hand beater whip together the sugars, tahini paste, and coconut oil until they are creamy and fluffy. Beat in the vanilla extract and soy milk.
- In a small kitchen, bowl whisks together the baking powder and soda, cornstarch, sea salt, and all-purpose flour. Once combined stir the flour mixture into the tahini and oil mixture just until

incorporated, being careful to not over mix. Gently fold in the chopped chocolate.

- Place the cookie dough in the fridge to chill for thirty minutes. Meanwhile, allow the oven to preheat to a temperature of Fahrenheit three-hundred and fifty degrees and line a cooking sheet with kitchen parchment.

- Scoop out the dough into two tablespoon portion sizes, preferably using a cookie scoop. You should be left with about a dozen cookies. Place these cookie dough balls onto the prepared baking sheet, each three inches away from each other.

- Bake the cookies until the edges are beginning to set and turn golden about twelve to thirteen minutes. For best results, turn the pan around halfway through the cooking process for even cooking.

- Remove the cookies from the oven and allow them to cool on the tray for two minutes before removing them to cool on a wire rack or a plate.

Double Chocolate Cookies

These double chocolate cookies are decadent and sweet, perfect to enjoy alone or with a glass of dairy-free milk. Enjoy making these cookies fresh, or you can prepare the dough ahead of time and store it in the freezer to have freshly made cookies on demand.

The Details:

- The Number of Servings: 12
- The Time Needed to Prepare: 5 minutes
- The Time Required to Cook: 10 minutes
- The Total Preparation/Cook Time: 15 minutes
- Number of Calories in Individual Servings: 227
- Protein Grams: 2
- Fat Grams: 10

- Total Carbohydrates Grams: 31
- Net Carbohydrates Grams: 30

The Ingredients:

- All-purpose flour – 1.25 cup
- Cocoa powder - .25 cup
- Baking soda – 1 teaspoon
- Sea salt - .25 teaspoon
- Baking powder – 1 teaspoon
- Vanilla extract – 1 teaspoon
- Vegan butter softened - .5 cup
- Soy milk - .25 cup
- Sugar – 1 cup
- Chocolate chips, dairy-free - .5 cup

The Instructions:

- Preheat your oven to a temperature of Fahrenheit three-hundred and seventy-five degrees and line a baking sheet with kitchen parchment.

- In a medium-sized kitchen, bowl uses a beater to combine the vegan butter and sugar until it is creamy and fluffy, and then add in the soy milk and vanilla.
- In another bowl, combine the baking soda, flour, cocoa powder, baking powder, and sea salt. Stir this mixture into the sugar mixture and once it is combined fold in the chocolate chips.
- Form cookie dough balls each with two tablespoons worth of dough, or with a single cookie scoop. Space the cookies on the sheet each two inches apart and then bake in the preheated oven for nine to ten minutes.
- Once completed remove the tray from the oven, allow the cookies to cool on the tray

for five minutes, and then transfer the cookies to a wire cooling rack.

Raspberry Shortbread Bars

These bars are quick and easy to make, full of flavor, and only require a few ingredients. This enables them to be the perfect option to feed a crowd, as everyone will love them. Enjoy them with the glaze, or melt chocolate over the top instead.

The Details:

- The Number of Servings: 12
- The Time Needed to Prepare: 10 minutes
- The Time Required to Cook: 55 minutes
- The Total Preparation/Cook Time: 65 minutes
- Number of Calories in Individual Servings: 346
- Protein Grams: 3
- Fat Grams: 19

- Total Carbohydrates Grams: 42
- Net Carbohydrates Grams: 41

The Ingredients:

- Coconut oil softened – 1 cup
- Sugar - .75 cup
- Sea salt - .5 teaspoon
- All-purpose flour – 2.5 cups
- Raspberry preserves – 1.25 cups
- Powder sugar - .5 cup
- Coconut milk – 2 tablespoons

The Instructions:

- Preheat your oven to a temperature of Fahrenheit three-hundred degrees and line a nine-by-thirteen inch baking pan with kitchen parchment.
- In a medium-sized kitchen, bowl combines the sugar, salt, and flour. Add

in the coconut oil and stir until the mixture is well combined and crumbly. Remove and set aside one cup of this shortbread mixture to use later.

- Press the remaining shortbread mixture into the bottom of your prepared pan until it forms an even crust, and allow it to cook in the oven for fifteen minutes. Remove the pan from the oven and increase the heat to Fahrenheit three-hundred and fifty degrees.

- Spread the raspberry preserves evenly over the pre-baked crust, then, crumble the reserved shortbread mixture over the top of the preserves. Place the pan back in the oven, allowing it to cook until golden and bubbly, about forty minutes.

- Allow the bars to cool for twenty minutes before transferring the pan to the refrigerator to chill for two hours. Once cold, remove the bars from the pan by lifting out the parchment paper and slice them into twelve even portions with a sharp knife.

- In a small bowl whisk together the coconut milk and powder sugar, and then drizzle this glaze over the sliced bars.

Pumpkin Pie

Whether it is Thanksgiving, Christmas, or just another weekend, you will find yourself loving this pumpkin pie. No holiday is complete without this iconic recipe, and now you can enjoy it better than ever and vegan! To top off this pie try some dairy-free whipped topping or whipped and sweetened coconut cream.

The Details:

- The Number of Servings: 8
- The Time Needed to Prepare: 10 minutes
- The Time Required to Cook: 55 minutes
- The Total Preparation/Cook Time: 65 minutes
- Number of Calories in Individual Servings: 210
- Protein Grams: 3

- Fat Grams: 7
- Total Carbohydrates Grams: 33
- Net Carbohydrates Grams: 31

The Ingredients:
- Vegan pie crust, unbaked, 9 inches – 1
- Pumpkin purees 1.5 cups
- Soy milk – 2 cups
- Brown sugar - .5 cup
- Maple syrup – 1 tablespoon
- Corn starch - .25 cup
- Vanilla extract - .5 teaspoon
- Allspice - .25 teaspoon
- Nutmeg - .25 teaspoon
- Cinnamon – 1.5 teaspoons

The Instructions:
- Preheat the oven to a temperature of Fahrenheit three-hundred and seventy-

five degrees and line a glass pie plate with your prepared vegan pie crust. Set this aside while assembling your pie.

- In a saucepan of medium size combine the cornstarch, brown sugar, and two tablespoons of the soy milk until there is a thick paste. Turn the stove to medium heat and then slowly pour in the remainder of the soy milk, whisking constantly to be careful and prevent clumps. Add in the pumpkin puree.

- While continuing to whisk allow the pumpkin mixture to come to a boil, reduce the heat to a simmer, and allow it to continue to cook until it is the consistency of a thick pudding. This process should take about three to five minutes. Add in the spices and maple syrup.

- Pour the pumpkin mixture into the prepared pie crust and allow it to cook in the preheated oven until it is set, about forty-five to fifty minutes. It will still be a little jiggly in the center of the pie, but shouldn't be liquid-like.

- Allow the pie to cool to room temperature and then chill in the fridge for a few hours before chilling. This will help the pie to continue to set up and is an important part of the process. Serve the pie as-is, with dairy-free whipped topping, or a drizzle of maple syrup.

Chapter 6: Beverages

In this chapter, you will find beverages to complement the plant-based vegan lifestyle. This is an important part of our diets that many people forget when making a change. They don't consider that coffee often has milk added, hot chocolate is dairy-based, smoothies often also contain dairy. To put it simply, many beverages contain non-vegan ingredients. Thankfully, you can easily make these drinks and more vegan! The number of dairy-free milk options ready to be purchased in this day and age is innumerable. While the options used to just be rice and soy milk, you can now also choose from almond, coconut, hemp, oat, and even compound blends of multiple kinds of milk together.

Golden Turmeric Milk

There are many benefits to adding more turmeric to your diet. This powerful compound has the ability to lower inflammation, increase antioxidants, treats depression, improves brain health, decreases the risk of disease, and much more! Whether you are enjoying this as a cold refreshing beverage in the morning or an evening tonic before bed, you are sure to love the flavor and benefits from this drink.

The Details:
- The Number of Servings: 2
- The Time Needed to Prepare: 3 minutes
- The Time Required to Cook: 0 minutes
- The Total Preparation/Cook Time: 3 minutes

- Number of Calories in Individual Servings: 169
- Protein Grams: 7
- Fat Grams: 4
- Total Carbohydrates Grams: 26
- Net Carbohydrates Grams: 24

The Ingredients:

- Dairy-free milk of choice – 2 cups
- Maple syrup – 3 tablespoons
- Ginger, ground - .25 teaspoon
- Cinnamon, ground - .25 teaspoon
- Turmeric, ground – 1.5 teaspoon
- Cardamom, ground - .125 teaspoon
- Black pepper, ground – .125 teaspoon
- Vanilla extract - .25 teaspoon

The Instructions:

- Combine all of the ingredients together in a blender or a cocktail shaker to ensure it is evenly combined.
- Serve the golden turmeric milk over two glasses or ice or heat it up on the stove and enjoy warm for a relaxing bedtime treat.

Maca Latte

Used throughout history in ancient India, maca can increase energy without jitters known to occur with caffeine. Not only is maca an energy booster, but it also improves mood, lowers blood pressure, decreases free radical damage, and improves memory, and boosts sexual and fertility health.

The Details:

- The Number of Servings: 2
- The Time Needed to Prepare: 2 minutes
- The Time Required to Cook: 3 minutes
- The Total Preparation/Cook Time: 5 minutes
- Number of Calories in Individual Servings: 207
- Protein Grams: 3

- Fat Grams: 13
- Total Carbohydrates Grams: 19
- Net Carbohydrates Grams: 17

The Ingredients:

- Maca powder – 1 tablespoon
- Almond milk, unsweetened – 1 cup
- Full-fat coconut milk, canned - .5 cup
- Turmeric - .5 teaspoon
- Cinnamon - .125 teaspoon
- Cayenne – pinch
- Cocoa powder – 1.5 tablespoon
- Black pepper, ground – pinch
- Vanilla extract – 1 teaspoon
- Honey, raw – 1 tablespoon

The Instructions:

- Over medium-low heat and in a small saucepan whisk together all of the ingredients. You want to allow the drink to get warm, but without coming to a boil. As soon as the mixture starts to simmer whisk it vigorously and then remove it from the heat and serve.

Tahini Hot Chocolate

With this rich and nutty hot chocolate, you will never miss dairy again. The tahini perfectly accents the cocoa powder, which is then perfectly sweetened with brown sugar. While there are many dairy-free milk options, this recipe makes use of soy milk, which most resembles dairy giving you the same creamy flavor you know and love.

The Details:

- The Number of Servings: 2
- The Time Needed to Prepare: 1 minute
- The Time Required to Cook: 5 minutes
- The Total Preparation/Cook Time: 6 minutes
- Number of Calories in Individual Servings: 238

- Protein Grams: 11
- Fat Grams: 13
- Total Carbohydrates Grams: 25
- Net Carbohydrates Grams: 20

The Ingredients:

- Soy milk, unsweetened – 2 cups
- Tahini paste – 2 tablespoons
- Brown sugar – 3 tablespoons
- Cocoa powder – 3 tablespoons

The Instructions:

- In a small saucepan whisk together all of the ingredients and allow them to come to a simmer over medium heat. Once it reaches a simmer, reduce the heat and allow it to continue simmering for a couple of minutes.

- Adjust the sweetness to your taste and then pour out the hot chocolate into two servings and enjoy.

Protein-Packed Green Smoothie

This smoothie is perfect for whenever you need to get all your nutrients but doesn't have the time or energy to cook. With this green smoothie, you get a selection of fresh fruits and vegetables as well as protein from soy protein isolate powder.

The Details:

- The Number of Servings: 2
- The Time Needed to Prepare: 3 minutes
- The Time Required to Cook: 0 minutes
- The Total Preparation/Cook Time: 3 minutes
- Number of Calories in Individual Servings: 323
- Protein Grams: 24
- Fat Grams: 8

- Total Carbohydrates Grams: 35
- Net Carbohydrates Grams: 25

The Ingredients:

- Banana, frozen – 1
- Apple, sliced – 1
- Avocado - .5
- Baby spinach – 1 cup
- Soy protein isolate powder – 2 cups
- Coconut milk, unsweetened – 2 cups
- Ice – 1.5 cups

The Instructions:

- Place all of the ingredients in the blender with the avocado, spinach, and apple in the bottom and the frozen ingredients on the top. By having the softer ingredients by the blades you allow it to blend more easily.

- Blend the mixture until it is creamy and without chunks. Serve immediately or store it in the fridge for up to twenty-four hours.

Conclusion

In this book, you have learned the recipes you need to begin a plant-based and vegan lifestyle. It may be a change, something you have been unsure if you can take on, but you are now prepared with the tools you need to succeed. If you begin your new lifestyle armed with these tasty, healthy, and simple recipes you will find that you attain all the success you have dreamed of. This lifestyle can be incredibly easy to follow, as you will never be deprived of delicious meals.

You can use the recipes within this book to enjoy your daily life, entertain friends, make holidays special, and much more. Who wouldn't love to enjoy Strawberry Oat Bars or Vidalia onion and Tomato Quiche for breakfast? If you are feeling a mid-afternoon lag why not enjoy some Oven-Roasted Okra or some Squash Fries and Garlic Chipotle Sauce? In the evening enjoy Butternut and Arugula Pizza or "Smoked" Carrot Dogs with a side of Creamy Avocado Potato Salad. After dinner enjoys a decadent slice of Pumpkin Pie or a Chocolate Chunk Tahini Cookie. Finally, you can enjoy your evening relaxing with a warm Maca Latte or Tahini Hot Chocolate.

With the plant-based lifestyle, you have new options you have never considered, new flavors, textures, and health benefits you have never been able to enjoy. However, you now have the ability to enjoy all of these and more.

--

Did you enjoy the cookbook? Do you want to learn more on healthy eating? Be sure to check my other books on Amazon.com searching for "Jessica Weil". Thanks!